Four Seasons

Original Poems and Responses to Classics

by Karen Greenhill

Also by this author: "**<u>Driven Crazy: A Female Trucker Dishes on Fun, Danger, and Quirkiness in a Semi</u>**"

karengreenhillauthor.weebly.com

If you enjoy this book, please review it on Amazon.com or Goodreads.com so others can learn about it – Thank you!

Table of Contents

Poems Written Before Age 20

The Mischief

By the river's edge in a forest glen
There's a little hedge that a fox lives in.
His fur's bright red, and his nose is cold.
There's a price on his head, but he's rather bold.

A coop raid last month with splattered fresh eggs
Inspired these hunts and a felled wooden keg
Left brew soaked in dirt, torn clothes on a line,
A Pekingese dazed, but all not mine.

So every morn' to dawn's awake,
A bowl of food and a crack in the gate,
Red coat of silk in the morning light,
I watch. He eats then takes flight

To my yard's brink where he turns and looks.
He seems to smile.
I am hooked.
Then he's run a mile!

Phases of the Day

Centered in an emerald forest
Where sapphire waters mirror green
Grows an ivory flower
So far from man not seen.

Dripping water, silent pool,
Echoing birds' call,
Greet the dawn's glory
By a rushing waterfall.

Tender stem with head held high
At an angle to face the sun,
Stamens with peach perfume
Ascend from throat of plum.

Under a swaying canopy,
Tracing an arc in the sky
Slowly throughout the day
Unseen by the watching eye.

Against a misted shadowed dusk
Hidden far from sight
In verdant foliage rests a bloom
Incandescent in the night.

Thorn Meadow

I came upon a meadow high,
Though meadow I should call it not,
And long on windy hill I stood,
Deciding if it were worth the walk.

Thorn bushes knee high covered the scape.
Yet the journey 'round seemed too far.
So I set forth with gentle care.
Thorns to create their eternal scars.

Partway through I looked back
And longed for a barren path.
Murmured curse then murmured prayer
Did nothing to ease the thorn bushes' wrath.

Then halfway through tired eyes felt drawn
To what lay among the thorns.
To my surprise a purple bloom,
Peaceful calm amidst nature's horns.

I reached the far side of the meadow that day.
A gentler attitude, I possessed.
Peace in mind though blood was shed
And blossom in hand I must confess.

The Smallest Things

One can find beauty in the smallest of things
Like the intricate canvas of a moth's dancing wings,
Or dust in sunbeams through a window nigh,
Or meadow blossoms as tiny as a robin's eye.

A universe of bubbles swim in a drop
Like the stars of a galaxy until they pop.
Each grain of sand born of volcanic smolder
On closer inspection resembles a boulder.

Each feather's composed of fibers galore,
And every plant's stem contains even more.
The veins on a leaf become microscopic.
So many things that miss being topic.

Tiny and tinier, teensy and wee,
Connecting together all that can be.
Infinitesimal objects passed over by all.
The wondrous things in the world that happen to be small.

Karen Greenhill

The Highest Wire

A bird lands on the uppermost wire.
What drove the small soul to go a bit higher
Than the tree beside the window
Full of birds that come and go?
What in the little creature's breast stirred
To give the wire such allure?
Attainments only call to a few.
Young fledglings could ask, "Is it me or you?"

Life's Music

You can hear it in a hillside stream,
In a thawing forest, in a lovely dream,

Or echoing from a distant bird's nest,
From sleepy hatchlings settling down to rest.

You can hear it through an infant's tears,
In the voices of those you hold dear,

Or the rush of wind through canyon or vale
Of whispering breeze or storming gale.

You can hear it in the crinkle of autumn leaves,
Or the drip and drop of icicled eaves,

Or the crunch of snow under stepping feet,
Or greetings shouted between friends in the street,

Or wind tossed tree limbs as they sway,
Or in the laughter of children as they play.

Karen Greenhill

Lost Thoughts

Forgotten poems have passed through my mind.
I didn't write them down at creation's time,
Gone now in the mist of former thoughts,
Never to be found once they are lost.

Surely others have ideas seem ideal,
Yet don't find a way to make them real.
The world must have lost a wealth of knowledge
That could fill the libraries of every college.

Have you an idea floating around?
Find pencil and paper and set it down.
Ideas do us no good abstract and loose.
We must draw them out and put them to use.

The Play's the Thing

The bard once said the world's a stage.
So I pose this question in verse:
If life's a play from age to age,
How come we weren't let to rehearse?

A Note So Shrill

Down my back a chill.
A coyote in the hills
Knows not how I feel
To hear a note so shrill.

The Humble Oak

Broad in girth,
Great in worth,
Rough bark like wrinkles of an agèd face,
Earthly beauty with majestic grace.
It's not without thought I pass the humble oak.
Endurance be its gift, though age be its yoke.

Karen Greenhill

Light Deep in Water

Rays of light through water,
I float in liquid state.
Above the afternoon feels hotter.
I float and think of fate.

All above is wrinkled sea,
And burgeoning boat's small hull.
Down here is heavenly hush
While above winds give no lull.

Gorgeous blue goes on and on.
I look and see nothing more.
I am the ocean's weak pawn
While above the waves still roar.

I look then up I rise toward air,
Through splendid rays of light.
I know what I've seen here is rare,
Lovely floating in the quiet.

Silence of Thunder

Beside a rushing woodland stream
I wrap myself in the silence of thunder
As wave against stone and wave against wave
Send up their roaring fury

Here I seek peace
Where it's loud it's quiet
And hope can be secured
Staring to waters with sun dappled surfaces

Today be gone and
Tomorrow here with renewed promise and comfort at last

I sit in brief reprieve
My mind dancing with thoughts and wishes
Hoping, reaching and searching for a future of peace

That's all I ask before I head back to painfully wait
I sit here in the silence of these thundering waves
And voyaging leaves and wish for peace

The Foals of Spring

The foals of spring
Are such curious things.
Their legs are like spindles
When at first they tremble.
They wobble to walk.
At a touch they balk.
They seem nervous despite
The strong mare at their side.

To think that they grow
From the grass that they mow,
And as slow as they run,
They'll be fast at a ton
When they frolic and charge.
One must say by and large
That these foals of spring
Are such curious things.

The River Runs Deep

We step out on the icy river,
Balancing carefully, all a-shiver.
We stand in the middle, oh so still,
And listen so quietly as to feel more chill.

Below our feet we hear the purr.
Under the ice, the water stirs.
The woods otherwise remain asleep,
While below the ice the river runs deep.

While trees stand quietly in silent slumber
The water flows unencumbered.
I think the woods have made a blunder
To be so still while the river thunders.

Karen Greenhill

The Simple Butterfly

Behold, will you please
The simple butterfly?
It flutters here and there,
As if it had not a care.

I do advise
For both me and you
That we pause, too,
To take in the view.

More than ours, their life is short.
But among flowers they play sport.
They linger then dash,
Living simply, yet with panache.

Can we not learn from those
Small simple fellows
Who stop and do not miss
A pause when it brings bliss?

Poems Without the Excuse of Youth

Interrogatives

What is goodness?
Is it really there?
Is it being kind?
Is it being fair?

What is mercy?
Have we really known,
If we've never seen,
If it's never shown?

What is love?
The most nebulous of all.
A value? A feeling?
A voice? A call?

Why then duty?
When so many fail
To hear the call
And follow the trail?

Why then faith?
Aren't we meant to see?
Why have a mind
Just to make believe?

Why then humility?
Are we meant to cower
Doggedly low
And just pass the hours?

And what of pride,
In which many wallow
Carelessly harming others
Their goodness gone hollow?

And what of greed,
That makes some so grasping
To steal others' bread
Till their last breath's rasping?

And what of apathy,
Love's opposite face
Turning one's back
In open disgrace?

In each of our lives
We see some rain
Whether we're caring
Or cruel or vain.

And yet there is giving,
Being honest and true.
Is that not goodness,
When generosity is due?

And yet there is pity,
Seeing through another's face.
Is that not mercy,
When our mind takes their place?

And yet there is caring,
In real words and deeds.
Is that not love,
To meet other's needs?

One simply does,
As one's meant to do,
For family and friends,
As they do, too.

One simply believes
That a human life matters.
No tenet should harm,
Nor cause to shatter.

One simply is
Imbued with an essence
Of universal power,
Of indefinable presence.

There is no one else
To credit or blame,
Yet the power of good
Still remains all the same.

Muddy Paws and Innocence

A run on the beach
Wind in hair
Tongue hanging out
Keen eyes darting everywhere
Exploring nose-first among rocks and pools

Unrepentant joy
Eloquent though mute
Elemental
Telling reverberations
Reaching the heartstrings of the universe

Muddy paws and innocence
We sit together and exchange looks
In that way we do, as friends such as us, remind each other
Of all that matters in the world
The most important is simple love

Friends

When we laughed for the same reasons
When you spoke your mind and let me do the same
When you were kind to me despite my flaws
That's when I knew we were friends

Karen Greenhill

The Master's At Rest

(England, an Edwardian household, the cook speaks)

Hush! The master's at rest in the alcove this morning.
    Didn't make it to bed last night, I see.
    A bit of drink?
    The ones who say they don't can be the worst.
Betsy, mind you don't brush against the curtain too strong.
The sound might wake him.

Should never have put that couch in there.
    Speak up, girl. No need to whisper so's I can't hear you.
    No. Don't pour him a cuppa.
    Leave him be. If he's resting good, I'm 'appy.
We'll get on with the cooking and cleaning quiet as mice.
Such a cold and thoughtless man.

It'll be good practice for you, Betsy,
    Not to clatter so with the pots and pans.
    Clanging and banging.
    It's enough to wake the dead.
Andrew, pop down to the basement and unlatch the chute.
The coal man's arrived.

And tell him not to come in here
    With his mucky boots on my clean floor.
    The master discharged the account in town.
    He told me himself yesterday morning.
Be quiet on your way and come right back.
We've work to do.

No sense asking, I suppose,
    What he wants to go and do that for,
    When he's got proper digs upstairs.
    Betsy! Those pans! I expect you've woken him now.
Not that I mind having to be so quiet
When we've got so much on for today.

The master walked home from the churchyard yesterday.
    Seemed to be feeling the cold.
    Well, it is a bit colder these November evenings.
    A body wants a wrap.
 Didn't bother climbing the stairs.
Such a lax and lazy man.

Betsy, help me set the breakfast table.
    We must be getting on with things, any road.
    He must have been awfully tired
    To stop so long down here.
What do you mean, Betsy, that he wasn't himself,
Last night while you were finishing the washing up?

He said he didn't think he could make the stairs?
    Why didn't you say, girl?
    Not that I believe in idle gossip.
    Enough of this chitchat.
The vicar is coming to supper tonight.
I've got more to do than stand here talking.

Although! If he was feeling ill,
    Maybe we should get a spot of tea into him, after all.
    Perhaps stave off a cold.
    Hope it's not a flu.
Pour it only half way, Betsy.
We don't want any spills.

What's the meaning of dashing my good cup to the floor?
    Be quiet, my girl!
    Contain yourself.
    Lord preserve us!
He's stone cold.
Fetch the doctor!

No! It's too late.
    Fetch the vicar.
    Andrew, you go.
    You'll get there faster.
The master is gone!
Such a good and blessèd man.

Mimosas

Economy of leaf and limb,
Part of family lore,
How misplaced you must have felt
Growing outside our door.

Long gray slender limbs
Surrounded by oak so good,
Near the ash and sycamore,
Beneath the towering cottonwood.

Limbs reaching for the sky,
Clean and free of moss.
Yet, marred by red ants digging in
And carved letters deep embossed.

To strike an attitude serene,
Tiny lobed leaves and brushy pink blooms,
A pose of coral sculpture seemed
To hover over dog day afternoons.

Our mutts dug nap-sized hollows
Around the base of your roots.
I climbed up high above
To sit in your arms reading books.

A bird of paradise lost
Among sparrows, jays and wrens.
A tropical bloom in repose
Amidst a temperate glen.

Karen Greenhill

Out Walking in the Sun

My bashful friend I know
Events so long ago
Pushed you to despair.
Then others left you there.
Outside of your control
A struggle for your soul
Long ensued and sought
Your essence to be bought.

Yet I have seen you live,
Always glad to give,
Humble with a laugh,
Knowing wheat from chaff,
Loving wife and mother,
Kind to many others.

Now you tell me sooth
That darkness has more truth.
I say to you, my friend
That I can see that trend,
But I call that insight there
And raise you with this here:

Those who appear as if in light
Yet lie and steal in spite,
Who laugh at others' pain,
As they only seek their gain,
Only seem to be in light,
Only seem to shine so bright.
It is ever they who fail
To see their wicked trail
Wend its way to black
Seldom to turn back.

Four Seasons

Like footprints in the sand
We know not when a hand
Keeps us from a fall
When all we see is walls.

So one can't always tell,
If life has felt like hell,
That the good side has won
Out walking in the sun.

But those around may sense,
May see the evidence.
Your goodness has rung true.
In real light. Was ever. You.

the tabby on the windowsill
(a villanelle, one of the most restrictive poetic forms in my opin-
ion, but thought to give it a go)

the tabby who was a stray
rests upon the windowsill
looking at the bright day

dreaming of a tiger's prey
the robin and the whippoorwill
the tabby who was a stray

such small goals you say
but he's seen no zebra kill
looking at the bright day

stripes show he holds at bay
the fierce hunter safe from want or chill
the tabby who was a stray

toy on the rug is his play
the killer with a gentle will
looking at the bright day

he rises, stretches, his rent to pay
a snuggle with his jack or jill
looking at the bright day
the tabby who was a stray

From This Place of Birth

A creature on a speck of dust
Spinning 'round a ball of fire
Sky gazing by day, by night
At starlight shining higher.

Noise and toil and busy life
All around on earth
Feels distracting looking out
From this place of birth.

The moon suspended in the sky
Floating quietly above,
Looks silent and alone,
As if deprived of love.

Sun and stars in violent flames,
Their placidity deceiving.
Who can blame our early kin
For spinning tales then believing?

It's all a bit too much at times
Being a creature of earth,
Looking out through space sublime
From this place of birth.

Elemental

The earth, the soil, the sandy shore,
From mountaintop to ocean bed,
The first on the ladder's rung,
From whence all come, To whence all led.

The water, resting on the earth,
From mist and drop, from stream to sea,
The second to mother earth has clung,
From whence all sated, from whence all flee.

The air, the wind, the breeze,
Skating over the sea so bleak
The third, of speech and all that's sung,
From whence all breath, to whence all seek.

The fire, the sun that rises and sets
Over all from dawn to eve,
The forth, the cradle of worship sprung,
From whence warmth, from whence belief.

Responsorial Poems

A brief explanation: The following section takes a look at a hand-ful of classic poems by timeless poets each followed by my humble response. I can't possibly fill the shoes of these giants, nor do I mean to try. So please regard this section as a celebration of the joy of reading and re-reading these authors' works. One of the remarkable things about poems is how, like holding a jewel and turning it to see all the delightful angles of light, these classic poems bear revisiting again and again.

The Fire of the Drift-Wood by Henry W. Longfellow

We sat within the farm-house old,
 Whose windows, looking o'er the bay,
 Gave to the sea-breeze, damp and cold,
 An easy entrance, night and day.

Not far away we saw the port,
 The strange, old-fashioned, silent town,
 The lighthouse, the dismantled fort,
 The wooden houses, quaint and brown.

We sat and talked until the night,
 Descending, filled the little room;
 Our faces faded from the sight,
 Our voices only broke the gloom.

We spake of many a vanished scene,
 Of what we once had thought and said,
 Of what had been, and might have been,
 And who was changed, and who was dead;

And all that fills the hearts of friends,
 When first they feel, with secret pain,
 Their lives thenceforth have separate ends,
 And never can be one again;

The first slight swerving of the heart,
 That words are powerless to express,
 And leave it still unsaid in part,
 Or say it in too great excess.

The very tones in which we spake
 Had something strange, I could but mark;
 The leaves of memory seemed to make
 A mournful rustling in the dark.

Oft died the words upon our lips,

As suddenly, from out the fire
Built of the wreck of stranded ships,
The flames would leap and then expire.

And, as their splendor flashed and failed,
We thought of wrecks upon the main,
Of ships dismasted, that were hailed
And sent no answer back again.

The windows, rattling in their frames,
The ocean, roaring up the beach,
The gusty blast, the bickering flames,
All mingled vaguely in our speech.

Until they made themselves a part
Of fancies floating through the brain,
The long-lost ventures of the heart,
That send no answers back again.

O flames that glowed! O hearts that yearned!
They were indeed too much akin,
The drift-wood fire without that burned,
The thoughts that burned and glowed within.

Karen Greenhill

Response:
Islands Would Drift by Karen Greenhill

Islands as on fire at night,
Flames reflect upon the sea.
Westward sun shining bright
Leaves deep shade upon the lee.
Shade that deepens into gloom.
Flames that flicker into glow.
Night stalks in like certain doom,
Chasing light till it must go.

Nighttime's sun begins to rise,
Lends her silver glow aloft,
Saving all from darkened skies,
Smoothing edges until soft.
Islands as in day stand still,
Peering at each other's shore,
Soaking in the sunless chill
Far into each lonely core.

Temperate and tropical,
Desert, jungle, tundra,
Unknown or famous, topical.
Alone or by the hundreds.
Stand as if far astray,
Waters lap on stone or sand,
Ocean, river, lake or bay,
Populated or unmanned.

Separated together.
Connected, yet apart.
Liquid as the sole tether,
Shore to shore and heart to heart.

31

The Chimney Sweep by William Blake

from "Songs of Innocence"

When my mother died I was very young,
 And my father sold me while yet my tongue
 Could scarcely cry ' 'weep! 'weep! 'weep! 'weep!'
 So your chimneys I sweep, and in soot I sleep.

There's little Tom Dacre, who cried when his head,
 That curl'd like a lamb's back, was shav'd: so I said
 'Hush, Tom! never mind it, for when your head's bare
 You know that the soot cannot spoil your white hair.'

And so he was quiet, and that very night,
 As Tom was a-sleeping, he had such a sight!—
 That thousands of sweepers, Dick, Joe, Ned, and Jack,
 Were all of them lock'd up in coffins of black.

And by came an Angel who had a bright key,
 And he open'd the coffins & set them all free;
 Then down a green plain leaping, laughing, they run
 And wash in a river, and shine in the Sun.

Then naked & white, all their bags left behind,
 They rise upon clouds, and sport in the wind;
 And the Angel told Tom, if he'd be a good boy,
 He'd have God for his father, & never want joy.

And so Tom awoke; and we rose in the dark,
 And got with our bags & our brushes to work.
 Tho' the morning was cold, Tom was happy & warm;
 So if all do their duty, they need not fear harm.

Karen Greenhill

And from "Songs of Experience"

A little black thing among the snow:
 Crying weep, weep, in notes of woe!
 Where are thy father & mother? say?
 They are both gone up to the church to pray.

Because I was happy upon the heath,
 And smil'd among the winters snow:
 They clothed me in the clothes of death,
 And taught me to sing the notes of woe.

And because I am happy & dance & sing,
 They think they have done me no injury:
 And are gone to praise God & his Priest & King,
 Who make up a heaven of our misery.

Response:
Once a Cherub by Karen Greenhill

Every dawn brings light and hope.
Sun beams slant o'er hills of green,
Touching every rock and slope,
Each lamb, shining, new, pristine.

Mothers call out to keep near
The newest to this wicked world,
Striving to hold their young and dear
Close by while cleaning coats of pearl.

Soon enough the world exacts
The price of wisdom from each youth,
Consequences of each act
Of fear or hatred or of ruth.

As through the streets little boys roamed
Calling sweetly; should break a heart.
To earn his keep so far from home
Each his life must map and chart.

Once a cherub, once a lamb,
But soon to be corrupted.
Abandoned by both ewe and ram
Once home life was disrupted.

"I can't go home again no more."
No one can unopen the box.
Life will make its scars and sores.
Brethren may scorn and mock.

Yet 'neath the hardened heart and skin
Each soul remains the same.
In deathbed he calls out again,
As if an infant, he makes his claim.

"I am innocent," he will say.
"I've never done no wrong."
But no one ever stays that way.
Therefore, we hear this song.

Death of innocence unlike guilt.
Experience borne, deeds done, words spoken.
Nothing stays straight in a world atilt.
Even cherubs may bear a heart that's broken.

Much Madness is divinest Sense by Emily Dickinson

Much Madness is divinest Sense –
To a discerning Eye –
Much Sense – the starkest Madness –
'Tis the Majority
In this, as all, prevail –
Assent – and you are sane –
Demur – you're straightway dangerous –
And handled with a Chain –

Response:
Amherst's Rose by Karen Greenhill

The lady of early modern prose,
Amherst's fresh poetic rose,
Aficionada of literary juxtapose.

Said to have led a sheltered life,
Because she never lived as wife,
Though she grew through time and strife.

Understanding beyond given credit,
To one living by grace of others' debit,
For their home and daily bread. It

Shows she saw beyond the everyday,
And with words and rhythm found a way
To voice thoughts others could not say.

Thus it became the spinster's plight,
Almost lost forever from light,
A deeply wise woman's insight.

Vision she knew deemed a danger
By any who thought it might be stranger
To leave her be than to change her.

The Road Not Taken by Robert Frost - 1916

Two roads diverged in a yellow wood,
And sorry I could not travel both
And be one traveler, long I stood
And looked down one as far as I could
To where it bent in the undergrowth;

Then took the other, as just as fair,
And having perhaps the better claim,
Because it was grassy and wanted wear;
Though as for that the passing there
Had worn them really about the same,

And both that morning equally lay
In leaves no step had trodden black.
Oh, I kept the first for another day!
Yet knowing how way leads on to way,
I doubted if I should ever come back.

I shall be telling this with a sigh
Somewhere ages and ages hence:
Two roads diverged in a wood, and I--
I took the one less traveled by,
And that has made all the difference.

Karen Greenhill

Response:
Way Leads On To Way by Karen Greenhill

Way leads on to way
The poet jests to say.

Life may seem a mere forward progression,
Or so roads look deep in our youth,
But each needs see some share of regression
To grow still closer to the truth.

Way leads on to way, most verily.
We often see in our life's track
Connections we think meant to be,
Going forward, then coming back.

Some say fear looks back and sorrow around,
But faith looks up, as if that's best.
Yet answers most often stem from looking down
At our own two feet to fulfill our quest.

The Way Through the Woods by Rudyard Kipling

They shut the road through the woods
Seventy years ago.
Weather and rain have undone it again,
And now you would never know
There was once a road through the woods
Before they planted the trees.
It is underneath the coppice and heath,
And the thin anemones.
Only the keeper sees
That, where the ring-dove broods,
And the badgers roll at ease,
There was once a road through the woods.

Yet, if you enter the woods
Of a summer evening late,
When the night-air cools on the trout-ringed pools
Where the otter whistles his mate.
(They fear not men in the woods,
Because they see so few)
You will hear the beat of a horse's feet,
And the swish of a skirt in the dew,
Steadily cantering through
The misty solitudes,
As though they perfectly knew
The old lost road through the woods...
But there is no road through the woods.

Response:
Carriage Through the Woods by Karen Greenhill

A carriage drew through a wood so grey
And down a limb sheltered path.
Horses spritely making their way.
Bare wheel tracks breaking the grass.

Distance hidden as if by smoke,
And on the grass a dew.
Suspended breath, pink cheeks, drawn cloaks,
Evening fog of blue.

Driver clicking to carriage steeds.
A young footman sights a deer.
Man and woman inside asleep.
Brooding doves sounding far and near.

As a carriage drew through a wood so grey
And down a limb sheltered path.
Horses spritely making their way,
Bare wheel tracks breaking the grass

Four Seasons Sonnets

Winter

The lord of winter has most patient come
And weaves his winds about the crystal sky.
The fields and forests embrace his kingdom,
And set the leaves and grit aloft to fly.
The deepest dark of night and cold will reign,
Amidst the winter's tide will be reborn,
As earth ventures far from the light again
Another sun to be both praised and scorned
Aged symbol of eternal life falls back,
And leaves earth's folk to contemplate their doom.
To teach his mother's children what they lack,
And make most grateful for the warmth of womb.
But hark! The pagan in the oak glade cries
And begs the sun with love to sympathize.

Spring

The virgin spring calls forth each leaf and bloom.
Sweet life blood quenches every wood and field.
Wild seeds are sown with mother nature's loom.
While open ground from winter's grip shall heal.
Each harrowed row waits for the coming grain.
Each field receives its bread of sacrifice.
The growing season through the wax and wane
Must bring the harvest forth, so pay the price.
Life's light draws nearer now and smiles again,
Warming earth's folk in early morning dawn.
More ancient oaths spout forth denying sin
Till fear of recompense is nearly gone.
The pagan stands on hill within the glen,
Chants songs of praise. The spells have worked again.

Summer

The prince of summer struts 'round haughtily,
Glorying in his youth and strength and heft,
Surveying all with lust and prideful glee,
Taking to heart the fruits of warmth and weft.
In brook and glen, in forests deep and dark,
Upon the windy moor, all 'round the earth
From village pulse to lost peak's calling lark
The land basks joyous in this time of mirth.
In full raiment the sun treads on the sea,
Tracing his ancient dance upon each wave.
Some folk say 'tis he who will ever be,
Encoding how each soul's breath can be saved.
The pagan revels in the glory time.
Upon the knoll he sings out at earth's prime.

Autumn

The mistress autumn plays her trolling harp,
Calling all to a fate of joy or doom,
Since all time answering to weft and warp,
Little knowing their path from birth to tomb.
The days will shorten and the nights grow cold.
Earth's folk toil at the harvest dawn to dusk.
Another year grown young and then grown old,
Another springtime's flowers turned to husk.
Once more the source falls back, but does not laugh.
The widow women glean the field in calm.
Strike the gong, herald the feast, kill the calf.
Let today's plenty be the soothing balm.
And, hark, the pagan at the sacred dell
Weeps tears of patient fear into the well.

Epilogue: The Four Seasons sonnets

I'd like to share my thoughts with you about the Four Seasons sonnets. Written in the English or Shakespearean style, they address the idea that early beliefs go hand in hand with human perception of the seasons and an erstwhile attempt by people to control their fate. I have included allusions to weaving, as early people believed the fates wove human destiny: survival, suffering, and attempts to comprehend the world around us thwarted by the haplessness of life. I see these sonnets thusly:

The first quatrain introduces an allegorical figure of the season. Female for spring sowing and autumn reaping. Male for the strongest, hot or cold.

The second quatrain looks at the human activities and natural occurrences associated with that season.

The third quatrain starts with the relationship between what the earth is doing in regard to the sun in that season, along with how ancient peoples could have interpreted it.

The last couplet focuses on an innocent pre-Christian called "the pagan" who represents early humans. He is closely associated with the land and how people tried to understand and even to manipulate their environment, believing, against all logic or scientific thought that perhaps it was through their supplications that the earth warms each summer and through their failings that it cools each winter.

I hope you enjoy these and all the poems presented here.

Also by this author: "**<u>Driven Crazy: A Female Trucker Dishes on Fun, Danger, and Quirkiness in a Semi</u>**"

karengreenhillauthor.weebly.com

If you enjoy this book, please review it on Amazon.com or Goodreads.com so others can learn about it – Thank you!

www.ingramcontent.com/pod-product-compliance
Lightning Source LLC
Chambersburg PA
CBHW031543060726
47590CB00004BA/1492